YoungWriters

My First Acrostic

The South & South West

Edited by Claire Tupholme

First published in Great Britain in 2010 by:

Young Writers
Remus House
Coltsfoot Drive
Peterborough
PE2 9JX
Telephone: 01733 890066
Website: www.youngwriters.co.uk

SB ISBN 978-1-84924-882-2

Foreword

The 'My First Acrostic' collection was developed by Young Writers specifically for Key Stage 1 children. The poetic form is simple, fun and gives the young poet a guideline to shape their ideas, yet at the same time leaves room for their imagination and creativity to begin to blossom.

Due to the young age of the entrants we have enjoyed rewarding their effort by including as many of the poems as possible. Our hope is that seeing their work in print will encourage the children to grow and develop their writing skills to become our poets of tomorrow.

Young Writers has been publishing children's poetry for over 19 years. Our aim is to nurture creativity in our children and young adults, to give them an interest in poetry and an outlet to express themselves. This latest collection will act as a milestone for the young poets and one that will be enjoyable to revisit again and again.

Contents

The Poems

George Humphries

G lorious
E normous
O rganised
R unning
G ood
E nergetic

H appy
U nderstanding
M erry
P erky
H ard
R osy cheeks
I nteresting
E ager
S illy.

George Humphries (7)
Blundell's Preparatory School, Tiverton

Freddie

F riendly
R uns
E ats
D ances
D oes well
I ntelligent
E ager.

Freddie Frankpitt (6)
Blundell's Preparatory School, Tiverton

Ellie Salisbury

Energetic
Likes Mummy
Loves Daddy
Incredible
Eyes are green

Sums I like
Ankle skips
Lively
Important
Small
Beautiful
Understanding
Rosy cheeks
Yummy food I like.

Ellie Salisbury (6)
Blundell's Preparatory School, Tiverton

Charles

Cool
Horrible
Annoying
Running
Likes football
Energetic
Skilful.

Charles Hutchinson (7)
Blundell's Preparatory School, Tiverton

William

Works hard
I am cheeky
Love my teddy
Likes Ellie
Intelligent
Animals I love
Mummy I love.

William Honey (6)
Blundell's Preparatory School, Tiverton

Rocco

Runs fast
Organised
Cares
Cooks
Orange juice I like.

Rocco Hartley (6)
Blundell's Preparatory School, Tiverton

Jon

Jolly
Organised
Nightmares.

Jon Robinson (6)
Blundell's Preparatory School, Tiverton

Riyo Chuang

Races are great.
I love soccer.
Young children are fun to play with.
Oranges are great to eat.

Chocolate factory is fun to go to.
Hiccup, I've got hiccups.
Up the tree.
Auntie is fun to play with.
Nuts are lovely.
Get that pet!

Riyo Chuang (6)
Christ Church CE JMI Primary School, Barnet

Joe Knowles

Joe is funny sometimes.
Oranges are the best fruit.
Elephants are my favourite animal.

Kicking a ball is fun.
Number 10 is my favourite number.
Oranges are juicy.
Water is nice to drink.
Lollipops are nice to eat.
Elephants are big.
Sam is my friend and he is funny.

Joe Knowles (6)
Christ Church CE JMI Primary School, Barnet

Eleanor

Eleanor likes elephants
Lying on the sofa
Eating sweets on my bed
Alice is a good friend when she acts like a ted
Nancy is fun to play with
Ondia and Olivia are my friends
Running in the park and having fun.

Eleanor Dean (6)
Christ Church CE JMI Primary School, Barnet

Bridget

Blue eyes.
Red tongue.
I am peachy.
Digging is fun.
Gardens are fun to be in.
Ears help you hear.
Today is Friday.

Bridget Hogg (7)
Christ Church CE JMI Primary School, Barnet

John

John has two sisters
On Saturday I swim
Helping Mum tidy up
Never alone, never sad.

John Creswell (6)
Christ Church CE JMI Primary School, Barnet

Bastian

Bastian loves brioche
Apples are green
School is fun, it's the most brilliant place in the world
Today I will learn and play
I like eating ice creams
Ants are tiny
Nancy is cool.

Bastian Willicott (6)
Christ Church CE JMI Primary School, Barnet

Joanna

Joanna likes her mum.
Odeon cinema is my favourite cinema.
A sister would be my dream.
Nancy is my friend.
Nana is my favourite person.
Apples I eat every day, especially on Sunday.

Joanna Solden (6)
Christ Church CE JMI Primary School, Barnet

Katie

Katie likes kites
And I like playing hide-and-seek
Trees have leaves and I like leaves
I like eating ice cream
Every day I walk my dog come rain or shine.

Katie Scott 6)
Christ Church CE JMI Primary School, Barnet

Sophie

S ophie is a star worker
O ranges are juicy to me
P enguins are one of my favourite animals
H ot food is yummy
I love sausages for dinner
E ggs are yummy with soldiers.

Sophie Ingham (6)
Christ Church CE JMI Primary School, Barnet

Myrto

M y brother is my friend.
Y oung people are babies.
R ice is my favourite food.
T omato is my favourite vegetable.
O range is my favourite fruit.

Myrto Kaltsidou (6)
Christ Church CE JMI Primary School, Barnet

Alice

A t lunchtime the food is hot
L unchtime is excellent
I am cool because I have ice in my name
C oca-Cola I don't like
E leanor is my friend.

Alice Mansur (6)
Christ Church CE JMI Primary School, Barnet

Shaun

Shaun is sensible.
Home is my favourite.
Apples are my favourite fruit.
Umbrellas are my favourite.
Nuts are my favourite food.

Shaun Sadegian (6)
Christ Church CE JMI Primary School, Barnet

Ross

Runs all about.
Oranges are very nice.
Sweets are very nice.
Sun is nice when I relax in it.

Ross Helcke (6)
Christ Church CE JMI Primary School, Barnet

Cerys' Favourite Things

Charlotte Rogers is my best friend at school
Everyone in my class wears school uniform
Running faster and faster is really, really exciting
Yesterday my auntie Linda came to my house
Sometimes I like to dress up like a princess

Drawing pictures of my mum and dad is fun
Under my bed are all my favourite toys
Now I am four I can say the alphabet
Night-time my mum or dad reads me a story before I go to sleep.

Cerys Megan Dunn (4)
College Town Infant & Nursery School, Sandhurst

Vineet Subba

Vineet is my name.
I go to College Town School.
Naughty I am not.
Early I get up to go to school
Every day.
Tuesday is my football day.

Sunday is my best day.
Urshila is my mother's name.
Bijay is my father's name.
Both I love
Always.

Vineet Subba (5)
College Town Infant & Nursery School, Sandhurst

College Town

Come and play
Our school is fun
Look at our teachers
Look at us run
Enjoy our friends
Go and join the fun
Everybody smiles at the sun

To have some fun
On a special day
We love our school
Now come and play.

Harvey Mills (6)
College Town Infant & Nursery School, Sandhurst

Porterfield

Playing with my garage is what I like best
Outside playing at the park is great
Reading my school books is a lot of fun
Toy Story is my favourite film
Early in the morning is when I wake
Rebecca is my sister, she is great
Family and friends I love to see
Instruments I like to play
Every day is lots of fun
Love and cuddles from my mum
Day is over, it's time for bed.

Toby Porterfield (4)
College Town Infant & Nursery School, Sandhurst

Scarecrow

Scruffy funny character
Crows are scared of me
Always standing still
Run away birds
Eat your seeds somewhere else
Can't you see I'm still here
Run away from me
Oh no! they say
We are on our way.

Ellie Mae Kaufman (5)
College Town Infant & Nursery School, Sandhurst

Hallowe'en

Hallowe'en parties are great fun
All my friends like dressing up
Lots of scary ghosty noises
Lucky black cats miaowing outside
Orange pumpkins made into lights
Witches on their broomsticks
Eating sweets and chocolate
Everyone screaming and laughing
Now it's time for trick or treat.

Millie Beesley (4)
College Town Infant & Nursery School, Sandhurst

Rugrats Football

Football is nice
Our garden is my pitch
Our wall is my goal
The referee is my dad
Beating my sister's side
And winning the chocolate cupcake
Laughing at my sister covered in chocolate mud
Loving football because it's dead good!

Ryan Pyle (6)
College Town Infant & Nursery School, Sandhurst

All About Me

H appy all the time
I have a brother called George
C utting, colouring and painting are my favourite things to do
K itty is my cousin
M illie is my best friend
A t ballet we practise dancing beautifully
N anny and Poppa Flynn and seaside Nanny and Poppa,
they are my grandparents.

Bea Hickman (4)
College Town Infant & Nursery School, Sandhurst

Infants

I love my teachers
N ow this is why . . .
F irst they are friendly
A nd I hate to say goodbye
N ext they are helpful
T hey are funny and cool
S o that is why I love my school.

Max Mills (6)
College Town Infant & Nursery School, Sandhurst

Ghosts

Great big ghosts can be scary on
Hallowe'en night.
Orange pumpkins have scary faces.
Spooky bats and witches
Try to trick you and put
Spells on you.

Chlea Millard (5)
College Town Infant & Nursery School, Sandhurst

Garden

Grass grows in the garden
Ants play in the garden
Roses smell beautiful
Digging helps the flowers grow
Earthworms live underground
Night-time I water the garden with my daddy.

James Paul (4)
College Town Infant & Nursery School, Sandhurst

Socks

Smelly socks
On my feet
Comfy socks
Keep my feet warm
Super socks.

Samuel Newcomb (5)
College Town Infant & Nursery School, Sandhurst

Snake

S nakes are slithery
N asty snakes bite
A snake can hiss
K issing a snake would be horrible
E very snake sheds its skin.

Laila Dale (5)
College Town Infant & Nursery School, Sandhurst

Kiera

K iera Leigh
I s always
E ager and
R eady for
A nything.

Kiera Leigh Wright (4)
College Town Infant & Nursery School, Sandhurst

Our World

K indness costs nothing
I love the world I live in
A lways treat others nicely
N otice other people's needs
A ppreciate what you have.

Kiana Evans-Snelling (6)
College Town Infant & Nursery School, Sandhurst

Megan's World At 5

M y monkey has a funny nose
E ggs are my favourite breakfast
G ood girls are nice
A pples are yummy
N oddy is my toy.

Megan Ross (5)
College Town Infant & Nursery School, Sandhurst

Swim

S plashing in the water
W et as can be
I ce cold
M agic!

Esme Coles (5)
College Town Infant & Nursery School, Sandhurst

Cats

C ats are my favourite
A rchie and Henry are my cats' names
T hey like salmon
S ometimes they sit on my lap all day.

Isabelle Weston (5)
College Town Infant & Nursery School, Sandhurst

Terrible Tyrannosaurus

Terrible because he can rip you apart
Yelling loudly
Roaring fiercely
Angry as a bear
Noisy as a drum
Nasty to others
Often as annoying as my brother
Scary as a ghost
Active as a bee
Ugly as a pea
Raging temper
Unhappy as it cannot eat
Stomping up to me.

Finley Cox (7)
Colyton Primary School, Colyton

The Angry Dinosaur

Danger is David Dinosaur
Interesting to watch
Nasty to others
On its own
Strong as an elephant
Angry as a tiger
Ugly as a lizard
Ripping all it sees.

Wilf Dare & Owen Collier (6)
Colyton Primary School, Colyton

Ladybird's Life

Little bugs called ladybirds lurk on the bush
Aphids are what they are looking for
Dainty as they walk
Young ladybirds look for their prey
Black in colour
Interesting as they crawl from leaf to leaf
Red to show it's poisonous
Dotty so they stand out.

Milly Kendall (6)
Colyton Primary School, Colyton

Dolphin

Diving dolphin in the water
Ocean waves, rain pouring
Large in size
Pretty dolphin fishing
Hunting fish
Intelligent like Miss Hayes
Nice and shiny as a star.

Jessica Metson (5)
Colyton Primary School, Colyton

Tiny Cat

Cuddly as a soft toy
Amazing claws scratching
Tiny cat, tiny cat, where have you been?

Louise Hartnell (7)
Colyton Primary School, Colyton

David The Dolphin

D iving David the dolphin
O cean out in the sea
L aughing he was drinking tea in the sea
P layful in the sea
H elpful as can be
I nteresting things he sees
N ice.

Holly Sweeney & Tilly Robins (5)
Colyton Primary School, Colyton

Sad And Happy Dolphin

D iving in the ocean
O cean clean and cold
L aughing happily and merrily
P erforming happily and nicely
H appy feelings
I ntelligent on the inside
N ice on the outside.

Lenni Bashford & Charlie Widger (6)
Colyton Primary School, Colyton

Funny Cat

C ute as a baby
A ngry as a tiger
T errible at swimming.

Harry Williams (6) & Zachariah Brooker (7)
Colyton Primary School, Colyton

Dolphin

Deep in the sea
Over the rocks
Lightning fast
Pretty
Has a long tail
In the water
Never naughty.

Rose Dack (5) & Liberty Widger (6)
Colyton Primary School, Colyton

Zebra Zoo

Zoo is the zebra's home.
Eating grass all day long.
Bossy zebra is angry.
Runs fast.
Angry noise.

Christian Dart (7)
Colyton Primary School, Colyton

Seaside

S ea crabs waiting for people to come
and the crabs will pinch them.
E ating some corn from the barbecue.
A beach is a very nice place.
S ea can drown you when you go to the line.
I like hot sand.
D o you like ice cream?
E ating healthy will make you strong.

Leon Mustafa (6)
Greenwood Primary School, Northolt

Seaside

S tarfish was exploring in the sand.
E ating a hot dog.
A seagull was flying.
S un is glowing in the sky.
I was in the sea.
D own the waves.
E ve went in the sea.

Shay James (6)
Greenwood Primary School, Northolt

Seaside

S and in my toenails
E els in the sea
A mermaid in the sea
S ome seaweed in the sea and an
I ce cream van to eat from
D ads with their children
E ating ice cream cold.

Cindya Morris (6)
Greenwood Primary School, Northolt

Seaside

S tarfish is sitting in the sea.
E ating a chocolate sandwich.
A shell in the sea.
S and is soft.
I was excited about the seaside.
D oing a sandcastle.
E ating chocolate.

Bartek Zielinski (6)
Greenwood Primary School, Northolt

Seaside

See swordfish in the sea.
Eating delicious chocolate ice cream.
A dinner seaside is fantastic.
Sandcastles are fun.
I love playing in the sea.
Doing some arcade games on the sand.
Exploring the ocean.

Samuel Lowndes (6)
Greenwood Primary School, Northolt

Seaside

Starfish in a rock pool.
Eating crisps and ice cream.
A seagull is fighting.
Sun is glowing.
I'm splashing in the water.
Delicious ice cream.
Eating crisps.

Jayda Balwant Willis (6)
Greenwood Primary School, Northolt

Seaside

Starfish sitting on the sand
Eating chocolate ice cream
And I saw a killer whale and he
Said, 'I'm going to eat you up!'
I was swimming in the rock pool. After that I said,
'Done!' I only got a little bit wet.
Eating more ice cream after all that!

Jack Ranson (6)
Greenwood Primary School, Northolt

Seaside

Silver shiny shells on the beach
Eating a coconut
Annoying your friend as a joke
Seeing the Red Arrows
Ice cold sea
Doing challenges
Exploring the sea.

Cameron Paul (6)
Greenwood Primary School, Northolt

Seaside

Shells on the beach
Eating ice cream on the beach
A crab crawling on my sandals
Sunshine glowing in my eyes
I am lying
Down in the sand, and I can feel shells
Everyone is having fun.

Serena Opong-Peprah (6)
Greenwood Primary School, Northolt

Seaside

Sunshine glowing in my eyes
Exploring under the sea
Aeroplanes flying in the sky
Seeing the sea and mermaids
I see crabs following me
Doing handstands in the sand
Exploring lots of fishes.

Parkkavi Thillairajan (6)
Greenwood Primary School, Northolt

Seaside

Sunshine comes down on the sand
Eating a big chocolate cake with my friends
A starfish is on the hot sand
Sand is very, very, very soft
I swim in the sea
Digging in the hot sand
Excellent days are at the beach.

Keira Mistry (6)
Greenwood Primary School, Northolt

About Zoe

Zebras are my favourite
Oranges are sweet
Ella is my friend

Exercise is fun
Apples taste great
School is fun
Teeth are wobbly
Writing is cool
On holiday I like swimming
On the sofa with my DS
Dancing with Mummy.

Zoe Eastwood (6)
Hayesdown First School, Frome

Hallowe'en

H allowe'en is fun because you can get in your own costume
I have a cat costume at home, you get sweets
A dark sky because it is night-time
L ook at the fire, it is scary for children, it can burn
L ike fire, it's red, orange but yellow as well
O utside there are light colours, there is fire at the bottom of the grass
W hat a hot day at Poldin Lane
E veryone was screaming, shouting and sparks were flying
E veryone was dressed like a witch but my mum has got me a
cat costume
N o, I don't like fire, it will burn you, it's scary.

Kaisha Edwards (6)
Hayesdown First School, Frome

About Christopher

C hristopher
H aines is a
R eading star
I n
S chool
T hinks tortoises are exciting
O ctopus are slow
P opular boy
H e is a doughnut
E veryone loves doughnuts
R efreshing Christopher.

Christopher Haines (6)
Hayesdown First School, Frome

Skateboard

Skateboard
Kick
A pick or
Trick
Exciting
Brilliant
Olly
Aaron
Roll
Dude.

Bradley Brown (6)
Hayesdown First School, Frome

About Elizabeth

Every day I am good
Love school
I am six
Zoe is my friend
And I am in
Badgers at school
Eager to learn
Teacher I like
Happy at school.

Elizabeth Bryant (6)
Hayesdown First School, Frome

About Charlotte

Charlotte wants to be the special helper
Happy and smiley
Apples are my favourite
Really good at work
Lotty loves school
Our dad says
Thinks a lot
Tickles her brother
Every day loves school.

Charlotte Willis (7)
Hayesdown First School, Frome

About Tia

Tia is great.
I'm a special helper.
At school it's fun.

Smiling all the time.
My name is Tia.
I've got brown hair.
Terrific Tia.
Happy all the time.

Tia Smith (7)
Hayesdown First School, Frome

Ice Cream

Ice cream is icy.
Cream running down.
Every ice cream is cold.

Cold like ice.
Red like strawberry ice cream.
Eat ice cream
And very yummy.
My favourite ice cream.

Anisha Rose (6)
Hayesdown First School, Frome

Ice Cream

Ice is sweet.
Cream is running down.
Every ice cream is cold.

Cold like ice.
Red like strawberry.
Eat ice cream
And it's very tasty.
My favourite flavour.

Amy Lee (6)
Hayesdown First School, Frome

Animals

A nimals all speak the same
N uts are cool
I n the wild you can see a lot
M any animals are babies
A n animal can have spots
L ots have teeth
S ome prowl for food.

Isabelle O'Shea (5)
Hayesdown First School, Frome

About Phoenix

P erfectly handsome
H ome is boring
O n time to go home
E at all the time
N athan is his friend
I 'm a friend
X -rays are silly.

Phoenix Gadd (6)
Hayesdown First School, Frome

Jack

J elly and ice cream
A pple ice cream
C ooking pizza
K icking the ball.

Jack Eagle (5)
Hayesdown First School, Frome

Rabbits

Rabbits are cute and they love carrots.
All rabbits hop.
Bits of rabbit food fall into their fluff.
Bits of straw on the bottom.
In the night you can hear it.
Tied to the cage, it's their house.
Sitting in the cage there is a rabbit.

Elizabeth Peniket (6)
Hayesdown First School, Frome

William

Will he work?
Is he working?
Learn to be kind.
Learn to play games.
In his mind he thinks I am good.
Am good at writing.
Maybe brilliant?

William Ferguson (7)
Hayesdown First School, Frome

Fire Of London

Flames shooting in the dark sky and it started in a baker's shop.
Incredible flames in the dark.
Revolting stuff.
Everyone could not put it out.

Oliver Bown (6)
Hayesdown First School, Frome

About Joshua

Jumping Josh
Opposite to sad
School is great
Happy at history
Unhappy at homework
Amazing Josh.

Joshua James (6)
Hayesdown First School, Frome

About Thomas

Tigers in my bath
Hippos in my cupboard
Otters in my bed
Monkeys in my attic
Ants on my head
Silly, crazy, Thomas' house.

Thomas Chapman (6)
Hayesdown First School, Frome

Sweets

Sweets are yum
We are always able to eat them
Eating sweets always
Eat up
Tasty
Sweets are the best.

Charlie Cox (6)
Hayesdown First School, Frome

Sweets

S weets are colourful
W e eat them
E veryone loves sweets
E at them all up
T oo many make you sick
S ugar in sweets.

Sabrina Gale (6)
Hayesdown First School, Frome

Autumn

A nd it's Hallowe'en at night-time,
U se pumpkins at Hallowe'en in autumn,
T ime for the leaves to fall from the trees in autumn,
U se fireworks on the right day or night,
M ummy has some time to read a book to me when she is at home,
N o dad takes me to school.

Abigail Thorne (6)
Hayesdown First School, Frome

About Joshua

J umping is fun
O ranges are lovely
S ometimes Mum plays with me
H ave lots of toys
U sing my bike
A lways good.

Joshua Roberts (5)
Hayesdown First School, Frome

About Callum

Cally is a monkey
And a friend
Loves PE
Likes literacy
Unhappy about maths
Makes Lego spaceships.

Callum Derrick (6)
Hayesdown First School, Frome

Sweets

Some are tasty and nice.
What sweets do you like?
Everyone eats sweets.
Every sweet is good.
Two sweets are good.
Sweets are good.

Owen Peet (6)
Hayesdown First School, Frome

About Daniel

Daniel is handsome
Amazing and cool
Never gets his spelling
Is beautiful and kind
Excelling and
Lovely.

Daniel Hancock (6)
Hayesdown First School, Frome

About Nathan

Nathan is good at football
A good friend
Toys keep him busy and
Happy
A super boy
Never breaks golden rules.

Nathan Cummings (6)
Hayesdown First School, Frome

School

School is work and drama
Cool school
High school is cool
Often late for SATs
Often late for detention
Late for English.

Matilda Furniss (5)
Hayesdown First School, Frome

About Jacob

Jam is nice
Apples are lovely
Creating clocks is fun
On holiday I draw
Best at cleaning the car.

Jacob Burgess (5)
Hayesdown First School, Frome

About Freya

F riends are fun
R eading books in bed
E ating apples is best
Y ummy carrots
A rt is my favourite.

Freya Leach (5)
Hayesdown First School, Frome

About Layla

L ayla
A lways smiling
Y ummy and happy
L oves school
A mazing Layla.

Layla Thomas (6)
Hayesdown First School, Frome

About James

J umping on the bed
A pples are juicy
M en in the army
E lizabeth is bossy
S wimming is fun.

James Allen (6)
Hayesdown First School, Frome

Megan

M y brother is called Harry
E very day I am good
G ood at singing
A lways good at school
N ever horrible.

Megan Wright (5)
Hayesdown First School, Frome

About Abbie

A bbie is my name.
B eautiful Abbie.
B rilliant Abbie.
I am 6.
E ver smiley.

Abbie Hill (6)
Hayesdown First School, Frome

About Billy

B aking is fun
I am good
L ots of toys
L ike sweets
Y ellow pyjamas.

Billy Card (5)
Hayesdown First School, Frome

About Skye

S pecial friends
K eep my bedroom tidy
Y ummy cakes
E verything that's important.

Skye Fuller (5)
Hayesdown First School, Frome

Fish

F ishes are colourful.
I love fishes by their fins.
S melly fishes are gross.
H ide from fishes when they bite.

Joel Joshua Williamson (6)
Hayesdown First School, Frome

Fire

F lames are hot
I am scared
E veryone is
R unning.

Jack Haines (5)
Hayesdown First School, Frome

The Fire Of London

F lames shooting from the sky
I ncredible flames
R unning people everywhere
E veryone was frightened.

Max Holoway (5)
Hayesdown First School, Frome

Fire

F lames shooting across the sky
I ncredible colours, red, orange and even blue
R eally incredible sparks
E verybody wants to watch.

Bradleigh Meadows (6)
Hayesdown First School, Frome

Fire

F lames are lighting up
I t's hot
R ed, orange and green
E veryone is running.

Connor Griffiths (5)
Hayesdown First School, Frome

Dogs

Dogs like grass.
Out for long walks.
Get the ball.
Splash in the water.

Hannah Oddy (5)
Hayesdown First School, Frome

Fire

Flames are hot
I am scared
Red and orange
Everyone runs away.

Eddie Laye (5)
Hayesdown First School, Frome

Fire

Fire is dangerous
I am scared of fire
Red and orange
Every time it's red.

Bradley Evans (6)
Hayesdown First School, Frome

Chestnuts

C ollect them.
H ard, spiky cases.
E vil because they can fool anyone.
S eason.
T hey fall off the trees.
N uts.
U gly.
T asty.
S trange.

Abbie Bolt (6)
Hayward's Primary School, Crediton

Chestnuts

C hestnuts are
H ard, brown, yummy chestnuts
E ating roasted chestnuts
S piky cases
T asty chestnuts
N uts are yummy roasted
U nder the trees
T asty roasted chestnuts
S quirrels collect nuts.

Bailey Vodden & Sam Mason (6)
Hayward's Primary School, Crediton

Chestnuts

Chestnuts on trees
Hiding on branches
Eat them now
Spiky cases
To break
Now look at them
Under the trees
Tasty and yummy
Sweet nuts.

Adam Treen (6)
Hayward's Primary School, Crediton

Chestnuts

Chestnuts for you
Hot and roasted
Eat them now
Some are very yummy
Tasty
Nuts are healthy
Under the autumn
Trees
See them and collect them.

James Powlesland (7)
Hayward's Primary School, Crediton

Chestnut

C hestuts roasted
H ot and ready
E at them
S piky cases
T o crack open
N ow you can collect them
U nder the
T rees.

Charlie Rook (6)
Hayward's Primary School, Crediton

Chestnut

C hestnuts ready
H ot and roasted
E at them now
S piky cases
T o break open
N ow you can collect them
U nder the
T rees.

Jacob Jackson (6)
Hayward's Primary School, Crediton

Chestnut

C hestnuts are yummy
H ow do chestnuts grow?
E veryone likes nuts
S ome green nuts
T hey grow on trees
N ever sit
U nder chestnut
T rees.

Gabriel Steed 6)
Hayward's Primary School, Crediton

Chestnut

C hestnuts are
H ard and brown
E at them on Bonfire Night
S quirrels
T hey
N ibble chestnuts
U nder
T he tree.

Raven Wild (6)
Hayward's Primary School, Crediton

Chestnut

Chestnuts are
Hard brown seeds
Eat them hot
Salty and big
The chestnuts live on trees
Never sit on them
Under the
Trees.

Emily Gribble (6)
Hayward's Primary School, Crediton

Conkers

Collecting conkers.
Open prickly cases.
Near the tree.
Kick the conkers.
Empty cases under the tree.
Ready for you.
Smooth, hard, brown conkers.

Millie Knowles (6)
Hayward's Primary School, Crediton

Conkers

Conkers on string
On trees they fall down
Nice and brown
Kick them
Even play with them
Really shiny
Shiny and brown.

Charlotte Haslam (6)
Hayward's Primary School, Crediton

Leaves

Leaves, lovely leaves
Enjoying playing
Ants eat them
Very pretty leaves
Excellent leaves
Spiky green leaves.

Jasmine Larkman (6)
Hayward's Primary School, Crediton

School Trip

School trips are cool.
Crazy kids running.
Hot but happy.
Out of breath.
Outings are fun.
Lips opening and closing.

The children are going crazy.
Running very fast.
I went on a big climbing frame.
Perhaps it is time to calm down.

Eloise Allen (6)
Hillbourne School & Nursery, Poole

School Trip

School trips are fun.
Crazy kids playing.
Hot and happy.
Out of breath.
On the climbing frame.
Loving everything.

Trips are fun.
Running around.
I like school trips.
Playing with your friends.

Kiana Persaud (6)
Hillbourne School & Nursery, Poole

School Trip

S chool trips are exciting
C razy children having fun
H appy children on the climbing frame
O ut of puff
O n the spiderwebs
L ots of spiderwebs!

T eachers having fun too
R unning children
I like trips
P lease can we come again.

Emma Louise Newton (6)
Hillbourne School & Nursery, Poole

School Trips

S chool trips are fun
C razy kids are loud
H ot children run around
O ne child runs around
O ur playground is great
L ook down to us

T rips are fun
R elay race is there
I t was fun
P ut coats on.

Rebecca Crane (7)
Hillbourne School & Nursery, Poole

Sarah

Scared.
Anxious.
Really sad.
Absolutely sad.
Her branch was big.

Maxim Capel (6)
Holy Cross RC Primary School, Plymouth

Sarah

Sarah gets scared
And she gets nervous,
Refuses to leave her brothers alone,
Although she's quite friendly
He likes her being trendy.

Phoebe Bishop (7)
Holy Cross RC Primary School, Plymouth

Sarah

She is brave
Always loves her mummy
Really clever
And she is kind
Her mummy is brave.

Leah White (7)
Holy Cross RC Primary School, Plymouth

Percy

P ercy is brave
E verybody loves him
R eally good thinker
C an be sensible
Y es you can.

Lloyd Webb (6)
Holy Cross RC Primary School, Plymouth

Sarah

S he was worried
A nd anxious
R eally scared
A round the house
H appy and excited.

Aidan Gill (6)
Holy Cross RC Primary School, Plymouth

Sarah

S he's the big sister
A brave girl
R eally good sharer
A kind girl
H er mummy is brave.

Francis Barba (6)
Holy Cross RC Primary School, Plymouth

Percy

Perfect Percy.
Everyone likes him.
Really brave Percy.
Caring and loving Percy.
You are wonderful.

Ellie Coles (6)
Holy Cross RC Primary School, Plymouth

Sarah

She's the oldest
A brave owl
Really kind sharer
And she loves
Her mummy.

Joshua Cockburn (6)
Holy Cross RC Primary School, Plymouth

Percy

Perfect Percy
Everyone likes him
Really brave Percy
Caring and loving
You are wonderful.

Tallulah Confue (6)
Holy Cross RC Primary School, Plymouth

Percy

P erfect Percy
E veryone loves him
R eally brave
C ute and handsome
Y ou are always kind and nice.

Isabel Jarvis (6)
Holy Cross RC Primary School, Plymouth

Sarah

S cared Sarah
A nxious Sarah
R eally sad
A bsolutely sad
H er branch was big!

Mackenzie Anderson (6)
Holy Cross RC Primary School, Plymouth

Sarah

S ensible thinking.
A ble to cry.
R eally brave.
A ble to think Mummy and
H er brothers have come back.

Emily Bryant (6)
Holy Cross RC Primary School, Plymouth

Sarah

Sarah gets scared
And she gets nervous,
Refuses to leave her brothers alone,
Although she's quite friendly
He liked her being trendy!

Daniel Robinson (6)
Holy Cross RC Primary School, Plymouth

Sarah

She's the big sister.
A brave girl.
Really good sharer.
A kind girl.
Her mummy is brave.

Darren Cochrane (7)
Holy Cross RC Primary School, Plymouth

Sarah

She is kind
And she is brave
Really loves her brother
And she loves her mummy
Help her brother?

Rosie Tannou Bailey (6)
Holy Cross RC Primary School, Plymouth

Percy

Percy the furry owl
Eats worms and mice
Really nice!
Cheerful and friendly
Young owl.

Isabella Roberts (6)
Holy Cross RC Primary School, Plymouth

Sarah

Scared
Anxious
Really sad
Absolutely sad
Her branch was big.

Archie Gunning (6)
Holy Cross RC Primary School, Plymouth

Soldier

Soldiers have to stay still some of the time.
On their heads are bear skin hats.
London is where soldiers are.
Danger is coming!
I like soldiers who protect us.
Everybody is safe.
Rotten enemies are defeated.

Benjamin Holmes (7)
Payhembury CE Primary School, Honiton

Britain

Britain's queen is called Elizabeth.
Running is popular in Britain.
In Britain they play lots of football.
The British people like fish and chips.
And the weather can be wet!
It is a very nice place.
Never a dull moment.

James Eaton (6)
Payhembury CE Primary School, Honiton

Britain

British guards stay still as a statue
Rubbish goes in the bin
In London is the London Eye
The sea is fun
A little island
In Britain there are three different countries
No I didn't want to go shopping today.

Ellie Jade James (6)
Payhembury CE Primary School, Honiton

Britain

B ritish guards have to stay still.
R hys came to London with me.
I t is a busy country.
T o the top of the palace we go.
A nd see the Queen.
I nto Big Ben we go.
N ot on the London Eye.

Haydon McCance (7)
Payhembury CE Primary School, Honiton

London

L ondon is a very busy place.
O n the London Eye it is very scary.
N ever run in the road.
D aily I watch the boats on the river.
O ver the bridge we go.
N ow Big Ben chimes.

Rhys Spiller (6)
Payhembury CE Primary School, Honiton

Queen

Q ueen meets the soldiers
U sually she looks nice
E lizabeth likes staying in her house
E verybody smiles at the Queen
N ever go in the castle!

Jenson Ashley Goodland (5)
Payhembury CE Primary School, Honiton

Castle

Castles are what the soldiers guard.
A flag goes up.
Sun shines over the castle.
The Queen lives in Buckingham Palace.
London is the capital of England.
Elizabeth Windsor is the Queen.

Eleanor Eaton (5)
Payhembury CE Primary School, Honiton

Tennis

Tennis is a British sport.
Everyone likes tennis.
No one is sad.
Night-time is too dark for tennis.
I like tennis.
Special people love tennis.

Kai Waldron (6)
Payhembury CE Primary School, Honiton

Castle

Castles are real
And the guard let you in
Sometimes the flag is down
Turrets are good for fighting
Lots of soldiers guard the castle
England is a good country.

Flo Somers (5)
Payhembury CE Primary School, Honiton

London

London is the capital of England.
Only the Queen goes out on a special occasion.
No one is allowed in the Queen's castle.
Daily Big Ben dongs!
Only the brave go on the London Eye.
Next it is a trip on the river.

Cameron Bryson (5)
Payhembury CE Primary School, Honiton

London

London is the capital of England.
Only the soldiers have to stand still.
Never run onto London roads.
Don't go into the castle.
On the tube you can go to Big Ben.
Noisy buses zooming everywhere.

Lydia Gammon (5)
Payhembury CE Primary School, Honiton

Queen

Queen of England.
Usually the Queen is out!
Elizabeth lives in Buckingham Palace.
Everybody likes the Queen.
Not everyone is allowed to visit the Queen.

Karhys Flemington (5)
Payhembury CE Primary School, Honiton

Queen

Quite beautiful she is.
Usually she writes letters.
Every day she walks her dogs.
Early she wakes to drink tea.
Nicely she waves to the children.

James Crudge (6)
Payhembury CE Primary School, Honiton

Queen

Queens live in castles
Under the palace are lots of mice
Elizabeth is our queen
Every day the queen visits people
Not everyone is allowed in the Queen's castle.

Thomas Jack Mullin (5)
Payhembury CE Primary School, Honiton

Queen

Queen Elizabeth has soldiers
Up in the sky is a flag
England has lots of people
Eating fish and chips
Neighbours are kind.

Eloise Doble (5)
Payhembury CE Primary School, Honiton

Toys

T eddy
O ld
Y ou are lovely
S miley.

Isobel Thomas (5)
Pensilva Primary School, Liskeard

Toys

T inkle
O range
Y ellow
S quidgy.

Kyle Sobey (5)
Pensilva Primary School, Liskeard

Toys

T op
O range
Y ellow
S oft.

Holly Nettleinghame (6)
Pensilva Primary School, Liskeard

Toys

T inkle
O range
Y ellow
S ock.

Amie Davidson (5)
Pensilva Primary School, Liskeard

Toys

T eddy
O range
Y ellow
S oft.

Eleanor Wilton & Sienna Wright (5)
Pensilva Primary School, Liskeard

Crackling Crumbling Fire

F reaky, fast and flicks flames
I t's burning hot
R unning away
E scape, emergency, ringing.

Aimee Fanning (6)
Pensilva Primary School, Liskeard

Fire Excitement

Flames flicking hot.
I like fire.
Run, flee!
Exciting.

Jack Hicks (6)
Pensilva Primary School, Liskeard

Big Fire Poem

Fire, help!
It's boiling in this house.
Roasting fire.
Exciting but it's scary.

Matilda Cacchione-Firth (6)
Pensilva Primary School, Liskeard

Fire Fits

Fast
It's exciting
Roasting
Enormous.

Teagan Jones (6)
Pensilva Primary School, Liskeard

Exciting Fire Poem

Fire is exciting
It is very hot
Roasting fire burns
Exciting fire is fun.

Grace Averre (6)
Pensilva Primary School, Liskeard

London's Burning

Flames are dangerous
It is burning
Racing
Exciting.

Kyla Lawrence (6)
Pensilva Primary School, Liskeard

Exciting Fire Poem

Fire is hot and when you touch it, it burns.
It is dangerous because it can burn.
Run away from fires.
Enormous fires are scary.

Sasha Sapelkin-Tambling (7)
Pensilva Primary School, Liskeard

Exciting Poem

F ire is flaming hot
I t is really, really scary
R oasting fire
E scape from the fire.

Maya K C Cotton (6)
Pensilva Primary School, Liskeard

Fire Poem

F ire is hot
I t is scary
R eally nice
E xciting.

Kyle Rogers (6)
Pensilva Primary School, Liskeard

Fire Poem

F ire is creepy
I t is hot
R umbling fast
E xciting.

Leah Miles (6)
Pensilva Primary School, Liskeard

Excitement

F lames going up in the air.
I t is dangerous.
R un, rush fast.
E xciting.

Albert Cooper (6)
Pensilva Primary School, Liskeard

Fire Excitement

F ire is hot and spooky
I am scared of fire
R eally, really dangerous
E normous.

Lauren-Mae Davis (6)
Pensilva Primary School, Liskeard

Fire Poem

F ire is creepy
I t is hot
R eally, really scary
E xciting fire.

Chloe Northey (6)
Pensilva Primary School, Liskeard

Exciting Fire Poem

Fire is scary
It's boiling in this house
Roasting fire
Exciting, call 999!

James Vaughnley (6)
Pensilva Primary School, Liskeard

The Mystery Poem

Freaky and noisy
It is really sparkling
Remarkably hot
Exciting fire.

Grace Davidson (6)
Pensilva Primary School, Liskeard

Fire Flames

Fire, creepy and spooky.
It is exciting.
Really hot.
Extremely wonderful.

Rhiannon Hodge (6)
Pensilva Primary School, Liskeard

Fire Danger

Fire is hot, hot flames
It is dangerous and smoky
Roasting hot
Exciting.

Keelan Williams (6)
Pensilva Primary School, Liskeard

Christmas

Children have presents
Happy Christmas
Rudolph and his friend Santa
Ice skating
Santa brings all the presents
Trees have decorations and ribbons
Many people
All the children have their toy stocking
Santa gives presents.

Mark Pateepoh (6)
Rodford Primary School, Yate

Birthdays

B ring presents.
I cing on the cake.
R unning to the party.
T asty cake and Coca-Cola.
H ats in the party bag.
D ad lights the candles.
A fter we clear up.
Y ummy cake.
S tars sparkle.

Arron Siney (6)
Rodford Primary School, Yate

Christmas

C ome to see the presents downstairs
H o, ho, ho!
R eindeer wait for Father Christmas
I cicles drop down from the house
S anta is getting the presents
T insel is sparkling
'M erry Christmas,' said Santa
A ngels are crowding round the house
S tars are glancing at the world.

Aaliyah Ashfield (6)
Rodford Primary School, Yate

Christmas

Christmas time is fun
Have you been good?
Reindeer flying fast
Inside the presents lots of lovely things
Santa likes stars
Trees are covered in snow
Mary had Jesus
Angels sing lots of songs
Sweets in your stocking.

Emily Boden (6)
Rodford Primary School, Yate

Bonfire

Branches on the bonfire.
On the tree there are leaves.
Night-time is a nice time.
Fireworks are pretty.
It's fun.
Rushing fireworks.
Exciting night.

Geraldine Green (6)
Rodford Primary School, Yate

Easter

Eggs are chocolate and nice.
A broken egg I like.
Sometimes I get strawberry egg.
Then tie them up.
Easter is fun.
Resurrection is when Jesus came alive.

Kacey Streeter (6)
Rodford Primary School, Yate

Easter

Eggs are brought to children
All the leaves grow again
Sweets are hidden inside the eggs
Treats for everyone
Easter bunny comes
Remember Jesus.

Summer Devey (6)
Rodford Primary School, Yate

Ben 10

Brave
Eats to keep him strong
Never noisy

Tries to help people
Everyone cheers for him
Not a human but an alien.

Ben Wigmore (7)
St Andrew's Primary School, Cullompton

The Big Fast Track

F ast track
A big tractor
R epair when broken
M oving

M aking trips
A round the farm
C oming and going
H eavy and big
I mportant
N ever stopping
E xploring everywhere
S hiny when new.

Ben Coombes (6)
St Andrew's Primary School, Cullompton

Teddy Bear

T op star for soft fun
E ddy is its name
D oes some work
D oes some cleaning
Y ou are pretty

B ig feet
E asy to find
A friend
R eally nice.

Teoni Pike (6)
St Andrew's Primary School, Cullompton

Motorcar

Music loud
Open roof
Top speed-fast
Often big
Really fast
Cool exhaust pipe
Always in the lead
Really shiny wheels.

Bradley Follett (6)
St Andrew's Primary School, Cullompton

Game Boy

Games to play
And good picto-chat
Mums sometimes play with it
Every day I play with it

Bundles of fun
On the DS there is a screen
Your friends can help you on your file on the game.

Daniel Casley (6)
St Andrew's Primary School, Cullompton

The Toy Car

Colourful
And fast
Races on the road.

Felicity Hodges (6)
St Andrew's Primary School, Cullompton

Mermaid

M ade of plastic
E very day I put her brown crown on
R ed hair
M oves her tail
A scaly tail
I t has shells, starfish and glitter on her tail
D oes have pretty hair.

Rebecca Matthews (7)
St Andrew's Primary School, Cullompton

My Toy Spider

S o many legs
P retend to go down pipes
I nsects for dinner
D ark corners to play in
E normous webs
R eally fun!

Andrew Webber (6)
St Andrew's Primary School, Cullompton

Teddy

T hey are soft
E very day I take it shopping
D oes be kind to me
D oes play with me
Y our best teddy.

Chloe Land (6)
St Andrew's Primary School, Cullompton

Barbie Girl

B eautiful clothes
A nd flowery dresses
R eally fun to play with
B ut they get tired
I nto bed
E nd of the day.

Niki North (6)
St Andrew's Primary School, Cullompton

The Marble Run

M arble runs
A nd
R olling everywhere
B oring days are fun
L ook at them go
E xciting fun.

Keelie Pepper (6)
St Andrew's Primary School, Cullompton

Bratz

B ratz bag is lovely
R ainbow bag
A pretty doll to play with then I put her
T o sleep when she is tired
S pecial toy.

Elisha Hooke (5)
St Andrew's Primary School, Cullompton

My Favourite Teddies

Teddies are cuddly
Everywhere
Dress them up
Dancing teddy bear
Yellow jacket looks nice.

Hannah Ottery (6)
St Andrew's Primary School, Cullompton

Bratz Dolls

Bratz are fun to play with,
Really beautiful,
And their handbags are fantastic!
They have pretty hair and
Zillions of dresses.

Rebecca North (6)
St Andrew's Primary School, Cullompton

Teddy Friend

Talking teddies
Explorer bear
Dancing bear
Dress them up
You and me.

Niamh Shergold (6)
St Andrew's Primary School, Cullompton

My Bratz Doll

B eautiful
R ainbow colours
A lways fun
T oys to play with
S weet dolls.

Faye Clapp (6)
St Andrew's Primary School, Cullompton

Bikes

B ig suspension
I s a great thing to play with
K nocking over cones
E nforced to race
S tops under control.

Daniel McNair (6)
St Andrew's Primary School, Cullompton

Farm

F arming
A pples in the garden
R un in the field
M uddy all over.

Sam Greenslade (7)
St Andrew's Primary School, Cullompton

The Dolly Poem

Does crying
On and off
Lots of cuddles
Lovely.

Amelia French (5)
St Andrew's Primary School, Cullompton

Ball

Bounces around
Always does big bounces
Love playing catch with my friends
Like playing with my ball every day.

Jessica Searle (6)
St Andrew's Primary School, Cullompton

The Toy Rhino Crash!

Car crashed
And it blew up
Rhino blocked the road
Superman saved the day.

Callum Harris (6)
St Andrew's Primary School, Cullompton

Bike

B umping along on my bicycle
I n the field
K nocking over soil
E verywhere I go!

Lewis Bailey (6)
St Andrew's Primary School, Cullompton

Cars

C ars can go very fast
A good racer
R ace with my friends
S hiny paintwork.

Jack McGuigan (6)
St Andrew's Primary School, Cullompton

All Kinds Of Dolls

D octor dolly
O ld doll
L ion doll
L ittle doll.

Millie Spurway (6)
St Andrew's Primary School, Cullompton

Cars

Cool exhaust pipe on the back.
Awesome spoiler on the back.
Responsible racing driver.
Special paintwork.

Ross Mills (7)
St Andrew's Primary School, Cullompton

Lego

Lego is cool you can make
Everything
Good and bright towers
Often.

Jacob Kan (7)
St Andrew's Primary School, Cullompton

Cars

Cool exhaust pipe.
Awesome spoiler.
Racing
Shiny wheels.

Aron Small (7)
St Andrew's Primary School, Cullompton

Cars

Clean cars
A very loud engine
Really fast
Shiny paint work.

Joshua Milton (7)
St Andrew's Primary School, Cullompton

Doll

Doctor doll
Old doll
Lion doll
Light.

Madison Kibby (6)
St Andrew's Primary School, Cullompton

Cars

Cars can move with wheels
And they have a boot.
Riding on my
Seat.

William Moore (6)
St Andrew's Primary School, Cullompton

Vets

V ets is fun to play with
E normous and little animals
T he dog is brave
S ad pets.

Yasmin Sweet (6)
St Andrew's Primary School, Cullompton

Cars

C ool car because its got a spoiler
A nd noisy engine
R eally fast
S hiny paintwork.

James Perry (7)
St Andrew's Primary School, Cullompton

Doll

D oes have a plastic body
O ther people come round to play
L oves to play with my friend and me
L ong blonde hair.

Jodie Peek (6)
St Andrew's Primary School, Cullompton

Ball

B ouncy
A ball
L auren it says
L oud when you drop it.

Lauren Peers (7)
St Andrew's Primary School, Cullompton

Ball

B ouncy ball
A nice ball
L ittle
L ike to play with it.

Genevieve Sarran (7)
St Andrew's Primary School, Cullompton

Cars

C an go very fast
A wheel nut is loose
R acing on the dirt
S mashing in to rocks.

Nathan Callaway (6)
St Andrew's Primary School, Cullompton

Doll

Does sit and stand
Others play with her
Like a friend to me
Lovely blonde hair.

Anna Bowles (6)
St Andrew's Primary School, Cullompton

Cars

Cool cars
Are fast
Really noisy engines
Shiny wheels.

Bradley Jones (7)
St Andrew's Primary School, Cullompton

Cars

Can go fast
And I play with it
Really fast
Shiny paint.

Logan Condie (7)
St Andrew's Primary School, Cullompton

Cars

C olour green
A nd fast
R aces all the cars.

Peter Ruth (6)
St Andrew's Primary School, Cullompton

Car

C ool car that shines
A shiny window
R eally awesome.

Ryan Ewings (6)
St Andrew's Primary School, Cullompton

The Car

C ars have wheels
A nd seats
R acing to the zoo.

Tamzin Broom (6)
St Andrew's Primary School, Cullompton

Dress-Up Doll

D ressing my doll
O range shoes
L ovely hair
L oves playing outside.

Melissa Jarrett (5)
St Andrew's Primary School, Cullompton#

Maddison

Minnie Maddie
Always hiding
Doesn't like painting
Doesn't like apples
I do like ice cream
Sleeping is my favourite
Often I like to draw
Never naughty.

Maddison Wilkins (7)
St Anne's CE Primary School, Weston-Super-Mare

Giraffe

Great big neck
It has brown spots
Really long legs
Always lazy
Face like a snake
Found in Africa
Enjoys eating leaves.

Phoebe Crane (6)
St Anne's CE Primary School, Weston-Super-Mare

Amy

All our mates can skip
My friends are nice
Yum, yum.

Amy Kent (5)
St Anne's CE Primary School, Weston-Super-Mare

Matthew

My favourite TV Programme is 'Horrid Henry'
At school I like maths
The teacher says I'm noisy
Telling jokes is funny
Happy
Excited
Wicked.

Matthew Emmery-Tabrett (6)
St Anne's CE Primary School, Weston-Super-Mare

Mothers

Magical cooking
Often takes me to the park
Thousands of cuddles
Helping children
Everybody
Really smiley
Super.

Chloe Matter (6)
St Anne's CE Primary School, Weston-Super-Mare

My Sister

Enjoys playing
Marvellous at gymnastics
Magical
Always happy.

Zoe Kroger (6)
St Anne's CE Primary School, Weston-Super-Mare

Dragons

Dragons breathe out hot fire
Roaring
And
Growling
Out in the wood
Noisy dragons
So big and strong.

James Smith (6)
St Anne's CE Primary School, Weston-Super-Mare

Monster

Mean monster
Outside my door
Noisy
Scary
Taping the door
Eating flies
Roaring.

Curtis Newell (7)
St Anne's CE Primary School, Weston-Super-Mare

Nyah

Nice but not naughty
Yesterday I got a present because I was good
Apples are my favourite fruit
Hedgehogs are my favourite animals.

Nyah Ryder (6)
St Anne's CE Primary School, Weston-Super-Mare

Sports

S port
P laying with a football
O ver the climbing frame
R unning
T ennis
S kipping.

Louie Howling, Daniel Coombes, Maxwell Allsop (5) & Aiden Hemmins (6)
St Anne's CE Primary School, Weston-Super-Mare

My Friend Mollie

M arvellous friend
O ften dances
L ovely and kind
L aughs a lot
I nterested in puppies
E njoys making things.

Millie Mann (6)
St Anne's CE Primary School, Weston-Super-Mare

My Father

F riendly and helpful
A lways gives me kisses and cuddles
T rain driver
H appy
E xcellent at teaching me things
R eally strong.

Beau Lloyd (6)
St Anne's CE Primary School, Weston-Super-Mare

My Friend James

James is my best, best friend.
And he likes making things.
Me and James like running races.
Enjoy playing together.
Sometimes he is funny.

George Cook (6)
St Anne's CE Primary School, Weston-Super-Mare

Me

Messy eating
Artistic
Sleepy in the morning
Over excited
Never naughty.

Mason Haycock (6)
St Anne's CE Primary School, Weston-Super-Mare

Emma

Everyone
Makes
Me move
Around.

Emma Kroger (5)
St Anne's CE Primary School, Weston-Super-Mare

Joseph Weakley

Joyful and happy.
Obeys the teacher.
School is hard.
Eats lots of food.
Peas for my tea.
Happy and I help.

Wind in my eyes.
Eat lots of tomatoes.
Alex is my best friend.
Kite flying.
Like my daddy.
Eat lots of lamb.
You are nice.

Joseph Weakley (6)
St Anne's RC Primary School, Reading

Lara Tutty

Lovely girl.
Always helpful.
Really tidy person.
Aged six.

Tries hard.
Uses her imagination.
Toast is yummy
Toys are fun
Yellow is my favourite colour.

Lara Tutty (6)
St Anne's RC Primary School, Reading

Andrea Robayo

Always good.
Nice people help me.
Doing my work.
Really tidy person.
Ellie plays with me.
Ants eat leaves.

Run fast in school.
Only has one sister.
Beautiful and helpful.
Always helpful.
Young girl.
Only six and a half.

Andrea Robayo (6)
St Anne's RC Primary School, Reading

Kathryn Raj

Kind and helpful,
All I do is work,
The colour purple is my favourite colour,
Harry would be the name of my brother if I had one,
Running is my favourite sport,
Yellow is the colour of my giraffe,
Natalia is my best friend.

Rain makes my flower grow,
Anya is my friend,
Jemima is my friend too.

Kathryn Raj (6)
St Anne's RC Primary School, Reading

Tilly Walters

Tiny I am,
I am tiny,
Little but I am seven,
Like to play the piano,
Yellow is one of my favourite colours.

Water I like,
All I do is work,
Like my mummy,
Tilly is my name,
Excellent at piano,
Running I like,
Summer I like.

Tilly Walters (7)
St Anne's RC Primary School, Reading

Alex Mayers

A person called Alex M
Learn and listen
Easy work at school
eXcellent at work

Mayers
After school I go to Joseph's house
Yesterday I went to Joseph's
Earn certificates
Really good worker
School really rules.

Alex Mayers (6)
St Anne's RC Primary School, Reading

Anya Edwards

Aaliyah and Anya M are my friends.
Nice and kind.
You are nice.
After lunch we can go to the park.

Every week we go to school.
Daddy goes to work.
Wonderful teacher.
Animals are exciting.
Really tidy.
Daddy came back from work.
Sunday and Saturday are the weekend.

Anya Edwards (6)
St Anne's RC Primary School, Reading

Rhianna

Rhianna
Has
Ice skates
And
Now she can
Nearly do
Amazing acrobatics.

Rhianna Turner (5)
St Anne's RC Primary School, Reading

Matthew

M atthew
A lways
T iny
T oothy snakes
H e fishes for them all
E very time he
W akes.

Matthew Wooldridge (6)
St Anne's RC Primary School, Reading

Ciaran

C iaran is my name
I am nice and neat
A t school I
R un and jump
A ll day like a kangaroo
N ow I am sleepy, goodnight.

Ciaran Murtagh (5)
St Anne's RC Primary School, Reading

Emile

E nergetic Emile
M unches monsters
I n lovely
L avender
E ggs.

Emile Carr (5)
St Anne's RC Primary School, Reading

Daniel

Daniel likes dogs
And he likes cats and rats but
Not
Itchy dinosaurs
Even if they have
Long scratchy claws.

Daniel Crabb (5)
St Anne's RC Primary School, Reading

Thomas

Tricky Thomas feeds
Hungry
Owls
Marvellous moles
And
Sometimes slippery, slimy snakes.

Thomas Rotheray (6)
St Anne's RC Primary School, Reading

Jemima

Jemima is my name.
Eyes are brown
My mummy is 33.
I love to play the piano
My tummy is rumbling.
A girl called Rowen likes me.

Jemima Thompson (6)
St Anne's RC Primary School, Reading

Oscar

One of my sisters goes to school
School is hard
Cars are good for being late
Ants are tickly
Rocks are hard.

Oscar Hazell (7)
St Anne's RC Primary School, Reading

I Love The School

Isabelle

Lewis
Orange
Vase
Elephant

Toni
Holly
Elf

Sock
Carmen
House
Opera
Oliver
Luck.

Carmen Tao (6)
St Francis' CE Primary School, Falmouth

Sean, Dad, Grant

S is for the sun
E is for an egg
A is for alligator
N is for naughty

D is for drink
A is for apple
D is for digger

G is for gorilla
R is for Romeo
A is for athlete
N is for nice
T is for terrible.

Sean Burrows (6)
St Francis' CE Primary School, Falmouth

Trevarno

Trees to climb
Ropes to swing on
Eyes of peacocks
Vines everywhere
Adventure and fun
Reindeers in their pen
Nature is so much fun
Outside with my family.

Lewis Munden (6)
St Francis' CE Primary School, Falmouth

Dinosaurs

D angerous
I n the wild
N eeds food
O ld
S cary
A ttacks
U gly
R oars.

Kye Whitfield (6)
St Francis' CE Primary School, Falmouth

Dolphin

D ashes through the sea
O ver and under the waves
L ovely movements
P lays excitedly
H appily having fun
I n the air jumping
N oisy splashes.

Oliver Gumbleton (6)
St Francis' CE Primary School, Falmouth

Sam

S melly
A lmost always good
M y big brother.

Daniel Fath (6)
St Francis' CE Primary School, Falmouth

Brannon

Boy who wears glasses
Runs very fast
And has a friend called Lewis
Never gives up
Nothing is hard for him
On his pole pulls himself up
Never does he sit.

Brannon Misselbrook (6)
St Francis' CE Primary School, Falmouth

Brother

Brilliant
Ryan
Older
Trendy
Happy
Entertaining
Rude.

Holly Williams (6)
St Francis' CE Primary School, Falmouth

Toni

Toni is a tomboy
Only playing with boys toys
Never plays with dolls or babies
I always play with Action Man.

Toni Mowbray-Ward (6)
St Francis' CE Primary School, Falmouth

Rocket

R ock star
O pens
C orner
K ian
E lephant
T ruscott.

Kian Truscott (6)
St Francis' CE Primary School, Falmouth

Castle

C reepy
A ncient
S pooky
T errible battles
L ots of treasure
E nchanted.

Luke Daniels (6)
St Francis' CE Primary School, Falmouth

Leaves

L eaves are beautiful
E specially when
A utumn comes
V ery crackly under
E veryone's feet
S o let's walk in the park.

Chloe Edwards (6)
St Francis' CE Primary School, Falmouth

Jordan

Jolly
OK
Really sporty
Don't like onion
And grateful
Never been good with his homework.

Jordan Brown (6)
St Francis' CE Primary School, Falmouth

Horses

Home makes me feel happy
On my dress there is hearts
Run for Ruby Red the girl
Sneezing makes you wet
Even stars shine
Sense boys leave you excited.

Daisy Stevens (6)
St Francis' CE Primary School, Falmouth

Space

Stars in the sky
Planets
Astronauts
Craters on the moon
Extraterrestrial alien.

Molly Green (6)
St Francis' CE Primary School, Falmouth

Lacie

L ovely and kind
A nd she is beautiful
C aring and she is funny and
I s my sister
E ats lots of pizza.

Beau Johns (6)
St Francis' CE Primary School, Falmouth

Lily

L ily is fun
I like Lily
L ovely Lily
Y ippee for Lily!

Lily Mills (7)
St Francis' CE Primary School, Falmouth

Pots

P lants growing
O ver
T he
S hed.

Lauren Gray (6)
St Francis' CE Primary School, Falmouth

Friends

Friends with Joseph
Really great to play with
I like my friends
Even friends are lovely to play with
Never hurt friends
Don't forget your friends
Smile to your friends.

Jay Burden (6)
St Joseph's Primary School, Devonport

Friends

Friends are good to play with
Really make me laugh
I love my friends
Every day we smile at each other
New friends are brilliant to play with
Dancing and skipping all of the playground
Special friends to treasure.

Ellen Chalmers (6)
St Joseph's Primary School, Devonport

Friends

F riendly people
R eally great to play with
I like friends because they like me
E xciting to play with
N ew friends to share with
D o you like friends too
S o I like you.

Riley Scott (6)
St Joseph's Primary School, Devonport

Friends

F riends love one another
R espect each other
I like to play with friends
E nd the day playing with friends
N ew friends are lovely and helpful
D aytime is always good
S haring is good to do.

James Glasscoe (6)
St Joseph's Primary School, Devonport

Friends

Friends are good to play with
Really good to meet friends
It's good to play with your friends
Everybody likes to make friends
Natural to make friends
Don't forget to play with friends
Someone likes to make friends.

Owen Evans (6)
St Joseph's Primary School, Devonport

Friend

Friends make me laugh
Really great to play with
It's great to have friends
Every day friends make me smile
Never forget your friends
Don't forget to play with your friends.

Joseph Judge (6)
St Joseph's Primary School, Devonport

Friends

F riends are for sharing books
R eally great to play with
I t's brilliant to have friends
E veryone likes to have friends
N ew friends are great
D on't forget to play with your friends
S omebody who cares is a great friend to have!

Lola-Mae Cotter (6)
St Joseph's Primary School, Devonport

Friend

F riends play nicely
R eally brilliant to have friends
I t can be nice to play with
E veryone needs friends
N ew friends are fun to make
D o play with your friends.

Deniz Utku (6)
St Joseph's Primary School, Devonport

Autumn Poem

Apples are falling from the tree
Under trees you will see squirrels
The leaves blow around
Underground hedgehogs go to sleep
Messy wellies covered in mud
Now it is time to cut the crops.

Roan O'Connor (5)
St Joseph's RC Primary School, Malmesbury

Autumn Time

Apples fall off the trees
Under the tree animals build their homes
The leaves are turning red
Underground animals fall asleep
Misty mornings
Nearly Christmas, I am happy.

Toby Kershaw (6)
St Joseph's RC Primary School, Malmesbury

Autumn Time

A pples are ripe.
U nder the trees there are nuts.
T ime to turn back the clock.
U nder the trees there are foxes.
M y mum is busy making a cake.
N early Christmas.

Sophie Dickson (5)
St Joseph's RC Primary School, Malmesbury

Autumn Time

A pples fall off the trees
U nder the trees there are hedgehogs
T ime to harvest the crops
U nder the trees are crunchy leaves
M ummy is busy in the kitchen
N uts fall off the trees, off the trees.

Amy Dickson (5)
St Joseph's RC Primary School, Malmesbury

Autumn Time

A pples are red and juicy
U nder the trees there are foxes
T he leaves are red and orange
U nderground badgers build their homes
M isty days
N uts fall off the trees

Arthur Wicks (5)
St Joseph's RC Primary School, Malmesbury

Red Delicious

R ed juicy apples
E at them every day
D ig it and plant it

D elicious any way
E at them, they're very healthy.
L ovely and yummy to taste.
I like them very much.
C runchy, crunch, munch.
I love red apples so, so much
O h how I eat them after my lunch
U p high in the trees they grow
S weet red apples, such a healthy treat.

Grace Whitehouse, Arabella Whitehouse, Sam Perkin, Cody Veal, Samuel Bloomer, Charlie Smith (6) & Daniel Whiteway (7)
St Uny CE Primary School, St Ives

Apples

A s big as a brain.
P ut them in a pie.
P erfectly yummy!
L umpy and bumpy.
E at them off the tree.
S ave them for winter.

Cameron Cawley, Betsy Peters, Thea Pritchard, Danny Petre, Bayley & Taylor (6)
St Uny CE Primary School, St Ives

Granny Smith

Green apples.
Round and spherical.
Always hard and crunchy.
Never red.
Nice to look at.
Yummy!

Sometimes organic.
Marvellous.
I love them.
Tasty, juicy.
Hard to eat with wobbly teeth.

Ben Smith (7), Lucy Wodskou, Henry Jackson, Lamorna McGiff & Ellis (6)
St Uny CE Primary School, St Ives

Pink Lady

Pink Lady apples are juicy
I think they are really tasty
Nice crunchy sound they make
Kids like to eat them when they are ripe

Looks so shiny and smooth
Apples are sometimes
Delicious, yummy and healthy
You and everyone love to eat apples.

Isabella de Rozarieux, Nyana Morgan, Caitlin Hollis-Coulson & Jake (6)
St Uny CE Primary School, St Ives

Clown

Clown is clever
Little and big clowns
Orange eyes
Wonderful ice cream
Noses are red.

Anthony James (6)
Stamshaw Infant School, Portsmouth

Ophelia

On a bicycle riding
Plays on the swing
Has two pigs and twenty two piglets
Enjoys *everything* at school!
Loves Mummy and Daddy
Is always happy
And is fab at colouring!

Ophelia Cooper (5)
Stawley Primary School, Stawley

Ollie

October born
Loves Mum and Dad
Likes fish and chips
Is seen wearing a John Deere hat
Enjoys riding on a tractor.

Ollie Barker (6)
Stawley Primary School, Stawley

Harry

H olidays in Spain
A bby's brother
R ides a yellow bike
R ushes around the playground
Y elling come on!

Harry Norman (6)
Stawley Primary School, Stawley

Ollie

O n Friday he swims
L oves fish and chips
L ikes cycling along the canal
I n yellow wellies
E ats sausages.

Ollie Steele (5)
Stawley Primary School, Stawley

Ellie

E ats bananas
L oves Daddy
L ove Mummy
I s always helpful
E njoys trampolining.

Ellie Popplestone (5)
Stawley Primary School, Stawley

Jemma Thompson

J emma likes jumping jacks
E mma is my best friend
M usic I love
M aths I like
A mazing at dancing

T omorrow will be special
H appy and proud
O bedient; I follow rules
M ature and helpful to Mum
P owerful at running
S killful
O range is my table group
N ice and friendly.

Jemma Thompson (6)
Wildridings Primary School, Bracknell

Benjamin

B right at maths
E xcellent when I think well
N ever naughty on the carpet
J elly is my favourite
A nimals are great
M ilk is good in the morning
I ce cream is yummy
N icky is my friend.

Benjamin Lewis (6)
Wildridings Primary School, Bracknell

Ethan Brock

E xcellent at jumping and climbing
T errific at football
H ealthy eater
A mazing at maths
N oisy sometimes

B rave
R ocking
O K
C ool
K ind.

Ethan Brock (7)
Wildridings Primary School, Bracknell

Harvest

H appy when we pick fruit
A pples are yummy to eat
R emember Harvest Festival
V itamins are in all kinds of fruit
E xcellent for you
S unny days, cold nights
T ables outside.

Tiegan Wright (6)
Wildridings Primary School, Bracknell

Harvest

Happy, cheerful children
Are eating
Ripe apples.
'Very delicious!' they say.
Every harvest day they
Share
Together.

Jodie Cracknell (6)
Wildridings Primary School, Bracknell

Harvest

Healthy children
Are always eating nice fruit and veg
Ripe apples for everyone
Very good food to eat
Everyone should eat together
So that
They can share.

Libbi Green (6)
Wildridings Primary School, Bracknell

Dan

Down
Apples
Now.

Daniel Goddard (6)
Wildridings Primary School, Bracknell

Matthew

Magic tricks on Monday
Amazing at football
Terrific at rugby
Tricks people, cats and dogs
Healthy eater
Excellent at basketball
Works hard at school.

Matthew Greenaway (6)
Wildridings Primary School, Bracknell

Harvest

Helpful people
Are kind at harvest; they share
Ripe apples, pears and
Very nice oranges for
Everyone to
Share
Together.

Euan McNulty (6)
Wildridings Primary School, Bracknell

Sophie

S ensible at working
O range is my favourite colour
P ainting I like
H appy and funny I am
I ce cream I eat
E xcellent when working.

Sophie Locke (7)
Wildridings Primary School, Bracknell

Hollie

H ungry always
O ranges are juicy
L oves Mummy a lot
L oves Daddy as well
I ce cream is tasty
E lephants are cute.

Hollie Taylor (6)
Wildridings Primary School, Bracknell

Harvey

H appy everywhere
A pples are amazing
R unning fast at football
V ery, very chatty and always hungry
E xcellent at scoring goals
Y o-yo man on Sundays.

Harvey Collins (6)
Wildridings Primary School, Bracknell

Chloe

C areful at writing
H elpful to others
L ovely at swimming
O ranges and apples are yummy
E ggs and bread for breakfast.

Chloe Elsley (6)
Wildridings Primary School, Bracknell

Grace

G ood at drawing
R eally good at running
A nd at swimming
C an climb trees
E veryone I like.

Grace Williams (6)
Wildridings Primary School, Bracknell

Young Writers Information

We hope you have enjoyed reading this book - and that you will continue to enjoy it in the coming years.

If you like reading and writing poetry drop us a line, or give us a call, and we'll send you a free information pack.

Alternatively if you would like to order further copies of this book or any of our other titles, then please give us a call or log onto our website at www.youngwriters.co.uk.

Young Writers Information
Remus House
Coltsfoot Drive
Peterborough
PE2 9JX
(01733) 890066